Useful Chords

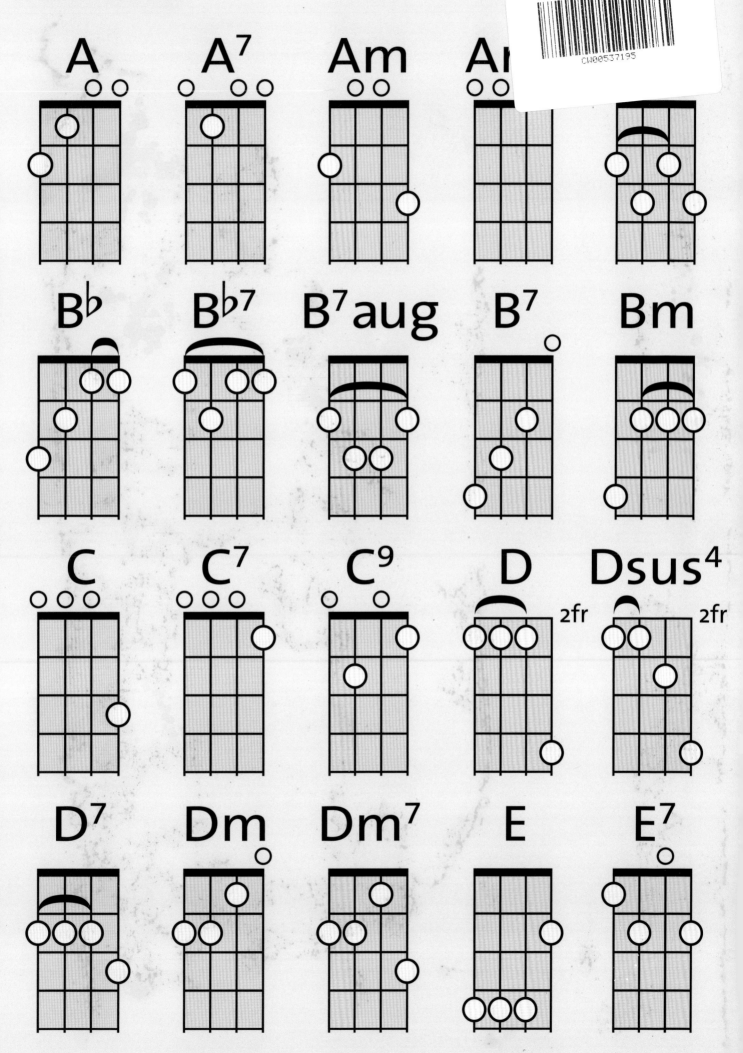

TUNING PEG

HEADSTOCK

NUT

FRETBOARD

FRET

FRET MARKER

NECK

G STRING

C STRING

E STRING

A STRING

ROSETTE

SOUND HOLE

BODY

BRIDGE

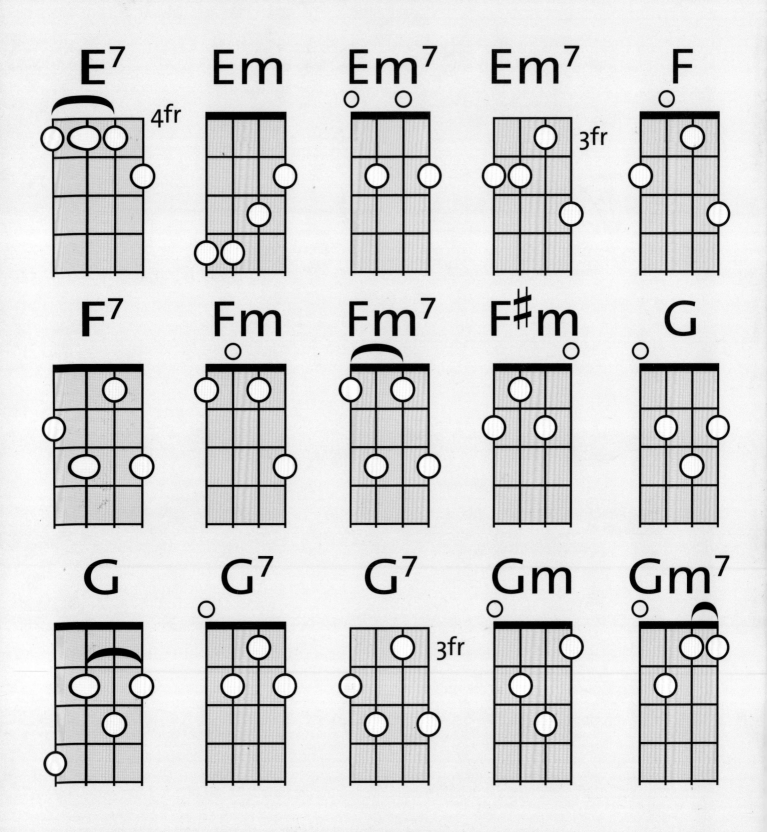

ISBN 978-1-78038-507-5

9 781780 385075

Chester Music
(part of The Music Sales Group)
Exclusive distributors:
Music Sales Limited, Newmarket Road,
Bury St. Edmunds, Suffolk IP33 3YB

Order No. CH79497
www.musicsales.com

CH79497
08/14
£3.99

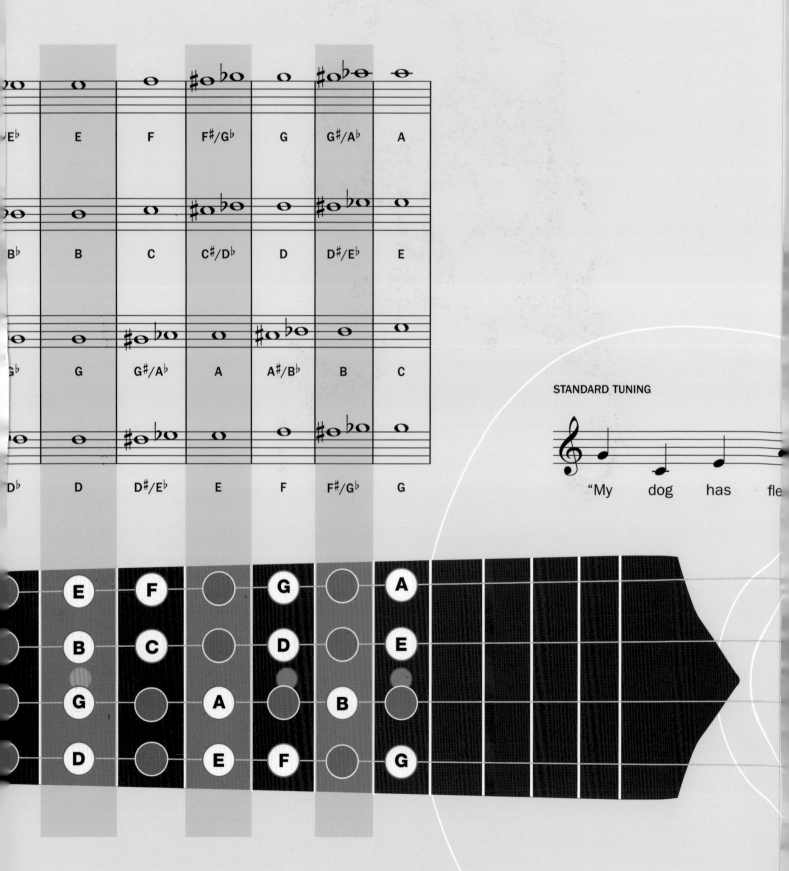

STANDARD TUNING

"My   dog   has   fle

Ukulele
Fingering Chart

With tuning notes,
chord shapes and a photo/diagram.
By David Harrison.

Ukulele Fingering Chart

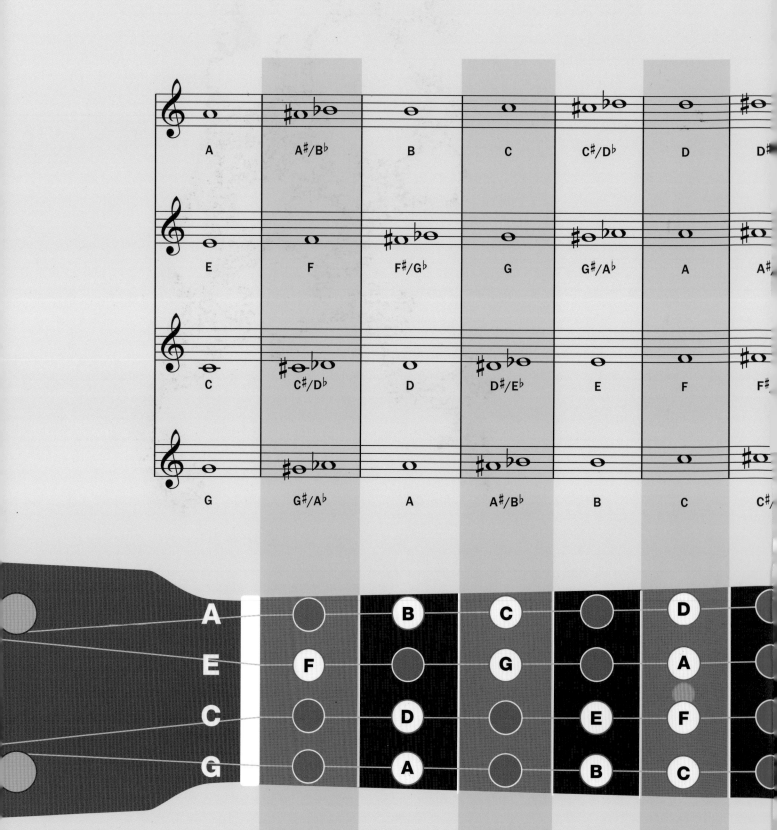